GW00568911

I COME FROM
A COUNTRY

I COME FROM
A COUNTRY
& Other Poems

Tijan M. Sallah

AFRICA WORLD PRESS

TRENTON | LONDON | CAPE TOWN | NAIROBI | ADDIS ABABA | ASMARA | IBADAN | NEW DELHI

AFRICA WORLD PRESS
541 West Ingham Avenue | Suite B
Trenton, New Jersey 08638

Copyright © 2022 Tijan M. Sallah

All rights reserved. No part of this publication may be reproduced, stored in a retrieval system or transmitted in any form or by any means electronic, mechanical, photocopying, recording or otherwise without the prior written permission of the publisher.

Book design: Dawid Kahts
Cover design: Ashraful Haque
Cover art: with the kind permission of the artist, Mahmoud Baba Ly

Cataloging-in-Publication Data may be obtained from the Library of Congress.

ISBNs: 978-1-56902-763-9 HB
       978-1-56902-764-6 PB

In Memory of Poets/Writer-Friends:

Dennis Brutus
Charles R. Larson
Atukwei Okai

Other Books by Tijan M. Sallah

Poetry Collections

When Africa Was a Young Woman
Kora Land
Dreams of Dusty Roads
Dream Kingdom: New and Selected Poems
Harrow: London Poems of Convalescence

Short Stories

Before the New Earth

Biography

Chinua Achebe: Teacher of Light

Ethnography

Wolof: The Heritage Library of African Peoples

Criticism

Saani Baat: Aspects of African Literature and Culture

Poetry Anthologies (Edited)

New Poets of West Africa
The New African Poetry
A World Assembly of Poets

Acknowlegments

The author gratefully acknowledges the following publications where some of the poems originally appeared in:

Remarkings (India): "I Come from a Country," "Ballad for Mom,"(revised to "Ballad for Mother," "The Red-Billed Hornbills of Coco Ocean," "The Wisdom of First and Last," and "Of India, I Have Hope for the Sun;
Poetry Wales (UK): "Faith Testing;" titled revised to "When the Sky is About to Fall;"
Black Renaissance Noire (US): "Elegy for the Sage of Katchikalli (for Dr. Lenrie Peters)" and "Dear Teacher (re-titled to "Elegy for Chinua Achebe")."

Some of the poems have been revised since their original publication.

About the Author:

Tijan M. Sallah, the Gambia's famous poet and writer, is known for his poetry and short stories, which appear in several major African and short story anthologies, including *The Penguin Book of Modern African Poetry* edited by Gerald Moore and Ulli Beier. He is one of Africa's most significant writers.

Contents

Other Books By Tijan M. Sallah   vii
Acknowlegments   ix
About the author   xi
Introduction   xv

I come from a country   1
Two things matter   3
In a tropical country   5
Questions and admonitions   9
On the road to Banjul   11
By the ricefields of Jeswang   13
Banjul   15
African Haikus   18
Ballad for mother   21
The red-billed hornbills of Coco Ocean   23
Yahmehxit/Jammeh-exit   25
Walls   27
Kotu Beach   28
The moth   30
Anansi   32
Slaying a Banjul crocodile   33
Gecko on the wall   35
A homeless person picks food from a
Washington trash-bin   37
The wisdom of first and last   38
Ode to Asia   40
Of India, I have hope for the Sun   44
Season of vengeance   46
Washington   48
Nasty palaver of Donald Duck   52

Midlife   55
Growing old   57
Come, be my friend   60
When the sky is about to fall   62
Elegy for Dr. Lenrie Peters   64
Elegy for Chinua Achebe   66
Elegy for Nadine Gordimer   67
Meditation on white hair   69

Introduction

These poems are about home and other places. But where is home?
Other places sometimes become homes. So where is home? Is home
necessarily where we have our roots or where we feel at ease. I invite
the reader to enter these miniature delights and frustrations to figure
that out.

--Tijan M. Sallah
Potomac, Maryland
March 17, 2021

I COME FROM A COUNTRY

I come from a country where the land is small,
But our hearts are big;
Where we greet everyone by name in the morning,
Blessed is the country where everyone knows your name.

When the sun rises and burns hot over our brows,
And the ocean rocks the shores, hurling memories and dreams,
We squint and open our arms with hope.
Blessed is the country where hope rises daily with the sun.

I come from a country where the river is our soul.
It transports our dreams and swallows our refuse.
It meanders like a snake, but is not hateful with venom.
At its head is brine; at its tail is sweet water.
Blessed is the country where you can eat barracuda at its head
And tilapia at its tail.

And the canoes come and go.
The ferries and boats traverse the frothy hill of waves.
And the fishermen spread their nests
To harvest wild colonies of mullets and *bonga* fish.

I come from a country where the land is small,
But our hearts are big;
Where poverty gnaws at our heels,
But we have not given up hope.
We continue to work.

And if resilience were a person,

She would live in my country.
She would be a calloused-handed woman
In sun-drenched rice-fields,
With a child strapped on her back,
But with a love enormous as the sea.

I come from a country where the land is small,
But our hearts are big.
Where we still believe in such things as
Sweating with your hand,
And still remember God and family.
And still support the indigent,
And carry Hope like oysters,
Sun-peeping from their shells.
Blessed is the country where people still find hope in the sun.

I come from a country where the land is small,
But our hearts are big;
Where poverty contorts the smiles of children,
But they still smile;
Where the sea is our strong ally against kwashiorkor,
Where men do not flood their entrails with coffee
To quench their civilized despair,
Blessed is the country where life still has zest and meaning.

TWO THINGS MATTER

Only two things matter in life:
When you were born,
And when you will die.
The rest is orange juice,
Or perhaps bitter kola nuts.
Up to age fifteen, you
Only think about your mother.
She has all the keys to your life:
Milk, rice, potatoes, beans;
Yams, cassava, *gari* and *fufu*,
And occasionally gourdfuls of beef and fish.
You don't want to cross paths with her.
Mothers can be gently ferocious
Like feral cats,
If you get too confrontational.
If you are wise,
You need to fill your heart
With love and obedience.

After age fifteen, you begin to
Think of girlfriends.
You have bypassed
The diapers and the belly stage,
You want more with your heart.
Pleasing the belly is no longer enough.
You may even try palm wine, or
Reach out for cigarettes
But such pleasures,
If not moderated,
Will hasten your end.

Unless you are strong
Like a wine bottle,
Alcohol will eat your insides
And dull your memory.
Cigarettes will corrode your lungs
Like acid.
And when you marry
And start gardening kids,
If you still partake and abuse alcohol,
It could even spoil your marriage, or
Buy you a homeless ticket.

Don't forget that
Only two things matter in your life:
When you started,
And when you will expire.
Where you started does not matter,
But when you started matters,
And when you end matters.

IN A TROPICAL COUNTRY

When you are airborne
And about to land in The Gambia,
You will see green distances of tall and slender palmtrees,
And houses with red and green tiled roofs,
And some with rusted corrugated
Or pyramid-shaped grass thatched roofs.
Do not think of it as picturesque;
Know that this is normal,
For you are arriving
In a Tropical Country.

As your plane approaches
Yundum Airport,
Which they incorrectly call Banjul Airport,
(You see, capital cities love to steal
All the good names for national assets),
You will see the airport is
White and geometric shaped
Like tiny white pyramids
Strung together, side by side,
Arms locked together in concert.
You will see a few decommissioned planes,
Lying abandoned on the old airport-tarmac.
These are all white elephants, or
Better called elongated silver elephants.
One is called Air Dabia,
Owned by a former deep-pocket Malian.
He was not so frugal;
So, he turned into a black elephant.

When you land on the airport runway
And your plane taxies to a stop;
In earlier days when there was no fence,
Pray that it was not raining
For you could then hit a cow.
The herders may even come to the pilot,
And say they are sorry,
That their cow hit your plane.
The herders had as much right to the land.

But these days when you taxi on the runway,
You will see airport personnel
And well-dressed welcoming folk
Slowly line parallel to the plane
Holding name-rich placards,
And ready to shuffle some government VIPs
And preferentially treat their luggage.
You know you are in a Tropical Country.
For in a Tropical country
Privileges outweigh merit.

When you descend from the plane,
You will smell the pungent smell of the bush.
In the welcoming crowd might be secret agents
Checking for those gadflies
That could unsettle the republic.
They look attentive and devious.
Do not give them any expression;
For they, like leopards, are trained to spot prey.
Just know then you are in a Tropical Country.

When you take the bus
To the main terminal, speak little
And listen much, for you are still
In the entrapment zone.
At the terminal, follow the line
But you will see some bypass the line

With handlers on their sides,
Do not do the same,
For you should know you are in a Tropical Country.
In a Tropical Country,
Order is for some; but disorder is for the elites.

When you see some
With their handlers bypass the line
And thrust their passports
Straight at the immigration officers
And you feel like protesting,
"Why should the last in be the first out?"
You should know you are in a Tropical Country.
Everyone knows Tropical Countries
Have juicy coconuts, and a hot sun,
And the hot sun fries the brain.
Or better still, the monied and powerful
Have big feet
And they trample, like dingy elephants,
Over the law and order.

When you pick your luggage,
Get some help from baggage handlers,
And please tip them generously
For they earn little because wages are low
And they have families
And need to keep their families alive.

When the airport gatekeepers
Ask to scan your luggage,
Please just comply.
Sometimes compliance
Can save you from a lot of palaver.
But when they want you
To open your luggage,
Please ask them, why? For why
Did they not even scan the

Luggage of the VIPs,
Who may be the biggest mob bosses in town?
Well, just know, this is how life is.
All trees are not of the same height.
This is how life is,
When you are in a Tropical Country.

QUESTIONS AND ADMONITIONS

I
Two white butterflies
In a circular dance
In my backyard.
Are they happy
They have seen sunflowers,
Or are they in love?

II
The African mask
In my sunroom is Kuba.
Copper and ivory decked on a face,
Or the muscular stern look
Of a famished king.
Which is which?

III
The lonely yellow butterfly
Flies so high above the mango trees
To the farthest reaches of the coconut trees.
What is its mission?
Some creatures seek their deaths
When they extend their reach.

IV
Squadrons of ants
Take over my floor
Like unabated floodwater.
Grains stacked on their heads,
As do refugees with their belongings.

Should I alert the ant-eaters, or
Call Pest Control, or, better still,
Should I simply let them be?

V
A Chinese man in Dakar
Complains his little boy loves
Senegalese food too much.
The little one joins the fishermen
In motions as they cast their nets
Into the turbulent waters.
I say, don't blame the little boy;
He has discovered one of
The secrets of Africa.

VI
The Chinese have discovered Africa
Under a deck of gold.
They also have seen the rosewood trees.
Please tell them,
We dislike barren landscapes.
We already have the Sahara.

ON THE ROAD TO BANJUL

Every time I drive from Sting Corner to Banjul,
I see tangled marshes of mangroves standing;
Their roots, thousands of curved legs,
Protrude so firm and menacing,
Like giant electrical cords.

The oysters hunt on their roots
With dark appetites; their mouths, like giant filters,
Crave for delicious plankton.
Occasionally, a baobab towers, with stems
Enormous as the shafts of hippos.
Tiny monkeys prey on baobab pods.
Amidst them, pelicans squirm around.
They form a white pageantry,
Like winged-cheerleaders.
The monkeys feast on fleshy coconut pods;
This landscape has become
Their choicest meal-island.

These monkeys play hide and seek
And sit on the crest of trees.
In their self-assurance,
They reign like the royals of the bush.
Their infants cling to their backs
With apprentice-appetites.
Give them time, they will graduate.
Like pirates, they will plunder rust and red
From every farm in the bush.

If humans do not intrude,

The monkeys are acrobats and gangsters.
They could suspend, on one arm,
On a baobab branch; their legs bent,
Dangling in the air, above the lush green undergrowth.
Then they could pull the other arm on,
To pedal along a branch
To a distantly located, forbidden fruit.

Perhaps these mangrove-marshlands
Are our Garden of Eden.
Every country has a Garden of Eden.
They remind us of the bounty that was
The Gift; how we squandered it
With disobedience and carelessness.
And how we, like monkeys now,
Forage, and then shudder from despair.

BY THE RICEFIELDS OF JESWANG

I saw women in swampy ricefields.
Half-buried to their waists,
They picked yellow tassels along interminable distances.
Rice grains, like yellow-hats on sentinels, protrude on green stems.
So bold the façade, and so noisy with uncertainties,
Like an impressionist painting.

The weaverbirds dived in and out,
Like fearful lovers.
They made lucky descents and ascents
Like nervous angels.
Scarecrows did not deter them.
In their daring feather-rituals,
They resembled a meteor-shower of invaders.
The fortunes of the peasants—they pecked at relentlessly.
"Hard to watch," a peasant said.
"Hard to countenance fearless thieves."
"Subookhum*! " the peasants said.
Scare-free, these birds,
Fortified like pirates in their conviction,
And undeterred by mannequins.

Rice stalks swayed to the wind,
And in thousands, they danced to the merengue of the wind.
Not mere choreographs, but actual tango dancers
With leafy undergrowth, resembling brownish green skirts.
Or was I obsessed with the leggings of women?

I saw women half-buried in swampy ricefields.
From their dresses, they resembled Jola women.
Stoically, they endured the scratch of thorns,
And the nuisance-sting of insects.
They picked weeds, piling them to dry,
And burned them, enduring the smoke.
I said to myself, these were the heroes of the country.
And blessed is a country that produces its own rice.

In the musty background, palm trees towered.
The *duk-duks* of pestles on mortars,
The practiced rhythms of women pounding grain,
Seized the unhurried normality of the day.

The Jola women knew that rice builds a country.
I wondered if they also knew that
So much of the country's fortunes depended on them;
That so of much of our survival
Depended on the grace of their coarse hands.

*   *Subookhum*: an onomatopoeia in Wolof meaning "good riddance."

BANJUL

I
Ah, in that decrepit island,
Shouldered by beach sand, wetlands, pine trees and mangroves,
The women wear bright *daagit* and *manaans** and flowing grand
    boubous*.
The daring women wear coral beads on their waists, the *ferri ndigas**,
Which they shake up and down:
Egal wachal, jotu mala talu mala*.

The men walk slowly pass the women;
Their worries weigh heavy on them like debt.
They chase after rice, cooking oil,
And school fees with stubborn intensities.
(Ah, such daily burdens can roast the feeble mind).
The young men seem not care.
They have their miniature worlds and assurances.
They kick soccer balls towards each other,
And exchange *behind-the-market* curses.

At the McCarthy Square, across
The broad stretch of green Bahama grass,
The youth play, and appear less worried
Because parents shower them with love.
They scream and shout like weaver birds.
They are oblivious to worry,
As long as their bellies are full.
For them, the day is
A savage run for pleasures,
An insane flexing of muscles to their hearts's full measure.

At the Tan-bi, this sprawling wetland
Of assorted mangrove and other hydrophilic shrubs;
At the end of Allen Street, the soil is dark and soggy.
Crabs, mussels, and cockle shells usurp the landscape.
Little crabs play hide and seek like little children.
Across, at the edge of the city,
The masts of ships stand imposing,
Like mobile monuments, like promontories.
Sea gulls fly above like salt-water angels.
Rusty corrugated roofs frown at them,
For being in a state of malice with paint.

II
Trade has a long history here,
Though I wonder, if it has lifted or sunk lives.
Portuguese and Dutch traders preceded the Arabs,
French, and British. They have left here
Droplets of language, designs, habits and manners.
The Portuguese left the word "*chave*;"the Wolof called it "*chaabi*."
"*Keys*" the English called it; "*le cle*," the French.
Who influenced whom? The mercantile debris
Is as mobile and fluid as the sea.

And the port of Banjul; it has known many brides of ships.
They all come to its quays to tie the knot.
It is a polygamous port.
Sail-driven local pirogues stare at it,
Wild-eyed with envy. And the dolphins,
Those local horsemen of the river, rustle
In whirlpools of tidal waves and froth.

This port has long been acquainted
To comings and goings.
But Banjul is still a decrepit island.
Most islands turn the gift of location
Into pots of gold or, if not gold, pots of silver.

Banjul seems to have done none of that.
It seems to have gone down, like an abandoned ship.
It wallows in the sleep of its history,
And has still not awakened boldly to the present.

The women still wear dainty grand *boubous*.
The roads protest vehemently, and are sad;
Their intestines are red, and spilled out.
The houses are rusty and sickly.
They have long been ignored; no one invests in their health.
Adamic landlords have abandoned homesteads,
And moved to the daintier Kombos*, or overseas.
They are now only absentees-in-chief;
They collect only the rent.
Mosquitoes are more aggressive now,
Because residents, more numerous,
Have more blood.

Banjul is a decrepit island.
My heart weighs heavy with pity,
Whenever I enter its gate.

*   *Daagit and manaan*:   In Wolof, woman's dress and loincloth.

*   *Boubou*: West African flowing robes.

*   *Ferri Ndiga*: Waist bead.

*   *Egal wachal, jotu mala talu mala*: Don't care for you; don't have time for you.

*   *Kombos*: the immediate area outside of Banjul, the capital city.

AFRICAN HAIKUS

I
Lean toads
In jars of water;
Their eyes, amber-like:
Ah, my poor neighbors!

II
Lice-rich ducklings,
In a pond; bathing;
Beaks, shiny wet:
Mom's first lessons.

III
Patient Anansi,
Sitting on yam leaf;
How did she create
The universe?

IV
This world is a jar-cup;
I drink and exit;
Brown cows drink
And exit.

V
Elephant tells turkey,
"I am bigger than you."
Big bird, angry, swells.

VI
If teardrops could
Convert to salt,
Cowards would become
The richest salt merchants.

VII
Owls, toads, chameleons,
We know your base secret.
You frighten
With your look.

VIII
I touched a lean tortoise;
Chicken crawled into shell.
Survival works!

IX
Calabash shrinks
To a gourd.
You forgot I like
More *nyama choma.**

X
Seagull surfs proudly
At insane depths of the sea.
Oh, fearless seaman!

XII
Down winding road,
Crows feast on an antelope.
Beware of speeding cars!

XIII
Shrill voices of beetles
Piercing the long ears of the sky.
The night blooms!

*   *Nyama choma*: East African roasted goat meat.

BALLAD FOR MOTHER

"I think continually of those who were truly great."
--Stephen Spender

Among the many greats I know,
My mother was truly great.
If your mind racks with doubt,
You did not know what I know about my mother.

She was a servant to relatives,
In ways only water knows against thirst.
She raised nephews and nieces;
She, mother-duck; we, her guarded brood.

Among the many virtues of her life,
Humility marked her routine.
Nephews and nieces called her *yumpagne**;
We, her blood-children, called her the same.

Although she was alien to the alphabet,
My mother was truly wise.
In the school yard of daily life,
My mother knew truth like a saint.

She taught us love with stories.
And made us fetch firewood and well-water;
Climb mango and guava trees for the harvest.
Of her many beliefs, hard work made the person.

She was a master at hygiene.
She kept our school uniforms meticulously clean.

She combed our hair; kept our fingernails short.
She oiled our skin with shea-butter; put *gonga* in our armpit.

Among the many greats I knew,
My mother was truly great.
If your mind racks with doubt,
You did not know what I know about my mother.

She never sailed the seas;
Yet, in her four scores of a life,
She was tuned to the world,
In ways only miracles can fathom.

She spent hours in the kitchen,
Braved wood- smoke and cinder.
She took care of our bellies,
In ways not even a royal cook can muster.

She was moderate in height and demeanor;
Her hands were rough with grace.
She spoke calmly and softly;
Patience found shelter in her heart.

We called her *yumpagne*,
She settled storms among uncles and aunts.
She was always in the middle with love.
She was water to hearts that were fire.

Among the many greats I know,
My mother was truly great.
If your mind racks with doubt,
I wish you had met my mother.

---

*   *Yumpagne:* in Wolof translates as "Aunt" or "Auntie." Because my mother raised our nephews and nieces who called her "Aunt" and were older, we her children followed suit with the same name, as a term of endearment.

*   *Gonga:* a powdery concoction of flowers with perfume smell.

THE RED-BILLED HORNBILLS
OF COCO OCEAN

First, I thought they were burglars,
But they can't be so daring at midday.
The sun was at its peak-climb, peering
Radiantly like a giant light bulb.
They kept assaulting my hotel-room window
With that strange repetitive constancy
That only robots or creatures of habit know.

Initially, I was hesitant to open the curtain,
To see the culprits behind the screech, the pecking.
But if not burglars, were they monkeys?
The hotel grounds were teeming with monkeys,
Tiny ones, with long tails like meerkats.
They were a bundle, adept at little mischiefs.
They climbed the Moroccan domes, the ornate hotel towers.
They chased each other's tails, fawning, frolicking. Or were they simply
Doing courtships like humans?

But the strange peckers at my window were not monkeys.
After a curtain pull—the surprise of their large, colorful beaks.
They were red-billed, white-breasted, with ashy wings, pied black.
How aggressive they can get—the window
Became a mirror to them. And they could not bear their self-reflection.
(It seems bird awareness is still corralled in instinct and habit).

The hornbills have not learned the lesson of mirrors.
Their outsized bills made them brave.

Birds with tiny beaks would have died
In an instant from such relentless pecking.
And it seemed they became more aggressive when they saw me.
Perhaps, in their tiny brains,
My presence made their self-reflection real.

Then I discovered a trick.
I closed the curtain and hid behind, making
Scratching motions like a mad man
To scare them off. It worked.
Perhaps their self-reflection then
No longer made sense.
I had warded off a nuisance.
Had I? The next day, they returned.

*   *Coco Ocean*: a five-star, beach-side hotel in The Gambia.

YAHMEHXIT/JAMMEH-EXIT*

The billboards speckled with white lies are gone.
The streets can now breathe; oxygen has come back.
The fear that paraded the land gave way to the sun.
The distrust of cousin to cousin is expelled
With the caftan-tail of the tyrant.

The mad rantings of a dictator are like an eternity.
They can weigh heavy, make a heaven boil like the fury of hell.
Suck green out of every plant; siphon blood from every heart.
But the yearning for freedom is like
The dogged path of the sun.
Come what may, it will rise over somber clouds
And lift up hope from our wretched fears.

This land has always been our land.
Tender shoots dreamed of turning
It into an Eden. We still had time.
The arithmetic of gloom coiled
Like a snake preying on the frogs of our land.
We tolerated its madness.
Many of our daring frogs got swallowed.

Humanity got railroaded bare;
It is the toy-game of tyrants.
The doors of heaven stopped
In the grand mansions of his indecorous pride.
Death sentences were made; poison-spells, carried out.
Tender shoots were trampled on;
Thunder struck fear in the land. We were left
To our mourning, as mangled bodies

Paraded with sorrow on every hamlet.

We knew we deserved better,
For we were children of sonorous dreams.
We knew we had the freedom of lions in us;
We just waited for the moment to seize hope.
A storm of disgust brewed in our hearts.
We only waited for the right window to strike.
And when we did, the whole world
Joined us in our boundless march.
The dictator fled in defiant consternation.
And the fearless streets cheered with hope
At what we had achieved.

Now we must not let freedom burn
In the chambers of complaints and complacency.
The detractors of freedom prey
On the unfulfilled pledges to the poor.
They are not dullards; they long for
The tyrant's return. We must not be fooled;
That history does not repeat itself.
But, damn well, it does, if
Those who guard the doors of liberty
Sleep like dunderheads at sunrise.

---

*   The poem's title comes from a congratulatory, if not celebratory, email that my
friend, Nobel Laureate Wole Soyinka, sent to me on January 26, 2017 following
the exit of the Gambia's brutal dictator, Yahya Jammeh, after a hotly contested
election. The title seemed like a pun on "Brexit." Jammeh had ruled Gambia
from July 22, 1994-November 6, 2017. In a subsequent email, Soyinka referred
aptly to Jammeh as the, "Maximum Ruler of Minimum Space," and noted,
"Let's hope the continent has seen the last of his kind."

WALLS

How can a country grow that erects walls?
How can it save its soul
If, once under a dim sky,
It needs angels?

What would have happened to *Relativity*,
If Einstein was put in a cage?
What happens to caged children
When you set them free?

The wire-nets are gone
But barbed-wires leave imprints on their souls.
Brains are scarred
By the cruelty of ill-intent.

How can a country grow that erects walls?
How can rabbits and deer feel happy
If you block their watering holes?
How can ranchers,
Border traders, border workers;
How can they breathe,
If you erect walls?

The eagles say,
Schadenfreude is the tool
Of little men:
Parochial dunderheads; unrepentant sadists.
So, they fly over in freedom,
Because eagles hate walls.

KOTU BEACH

I.
Every morning, the fishermen go out to sea.
The water is frenzied, lifting hydra-headed cobras,
Churning its writhing potential into menacing motion.
The fishermen slap their paddles
On sea-foam and waves, towards the deeper reaches,
While they sing songs of lobsters and oysters,
And blossom drunk from salty air.

Like rock-miners, they go into deep veins of water,
Searching for pelagic or demersal luck along coral reefs.
Their nets tunnel with hope
Through waters for a brimming catch.
Their pirogues display Rastafarian colors.
Some have graffiti, *Yalla baakhna**.
They brave the waves, while sea-gulls shit and piss over their heads.
Occasionally, luck bubbles up from the sempiternal sea.

II.
The Scandinavians are lying on the beaches.
They are lying butt-naked on towels on beach sand.
They are drinking Heineken and Beck beers
And wearing sunglasses to filter the blinding sun.
They are enjoying the street-boys riding horses on the beach sand.
They are enjoying the beach boys playing soccer in boxer shorts.
They converse with the beach vendors about their local crafts.
They are holding their flip flops.
They are treading bare feet on the sand.
They are enjoying games of flesh with young Gambians.
They are enjoying the freedom of a culture of watery rules.

III.
The fishermen are bringing back their catch.
They have harvested the luck of the sea.
There is a boy vomiting on the beach from sea-sickness.
There is a boy too new to harvesting fortune.
An old woman is tapping on his back
To empty his insides.
A young woman is holding sliced lemon
To help cure his ailments.
Lemon and salt are potent cures.
Lemon and salt are
The elixirs of the poor.

IV
The village women are waiting on the beach for the bargain.
They hold large bowls anticipating the catch.
They love most the *yaai boi*, the *bony fish*.
The *yaai boi* is the *fish of the poor*.
Fresh *yaai boi*, still alive, flip flopping in the boat.
They are delicious as the fishes of paradise.
People say, God planted the bones to ensure the poor can eat them.
Wise God, you always protect the poor—if only they knew!

---

*   *Yalla baakhna*: In Wolof means "God is good."

THE MOTH

I woke up to a blackish brown moth
On my window, fluttering, fluttering,
Between the glass and wire gauze,
In a pointless combat to get out.
Outside, the sun was rising, a phantom,
Behind the white oaks and pines.
The azaleas and *kwanzan* cherry trees
Dazzled guava yellow and red.

Unaided, the moth seemed more rattled to get out.
I kept watching it,
Fluttering, fluttering
Like a trapped wasp.
But it was not a wasp;
It had no instinct to harm.
It just wanted to get out.
And it seemed it saw the light,
But its brain was too small
To figure out an exit.

I thought of leaving it alone.
But I noticed that sometimes
Leaving some things alone may
End their fate.
So I tried to lift up the glass window;
But it still crawled helplessly
Across the wire gauze.
The light outside was greater attraction
Than the darkness inside.
It kept fluttering and fluttering

Doggedly on the wire gauze.

I decided to tear a piece
Of kitchen paper
And approached the moth
With father-love;
Seized it gently between
The folds of the paper
And walked to my door
And released it outside.

It flew so rapidly from my hand.
I felt then a moment of pleasure,
That on this day,
I have saved a life.

ANANSI

Crawl along, natural architect,
On the tiny bridges of your imagination.
I look out, and see you hanging on strings
Between the roof and the wall of the house.
They say, you are Anansi, the clever spider.

You can weave giant cobwebs
Between two baobabs,
And trap the unsuspecting butterfly
In your translucent net.
When it rains in giant pellets,
You can mend your nest
With the glue of your spit.

They use the word "genius" for humans.
But if genius is proportioning
Brain size to achievement, you are
A mightier "genius."
I would love to learn
The tricks of your genius.
Do you have hidden pliers?
Or tiny hammers?   Is the world
Of the little mightier than the large?

I would love to be a spider-apprentice
For a season.
And learn your brilliance
In the university of the tiny.

SLAYING A BANJUL CROCODILE
(for Ebrima Ceesay)

The children shouted, a lynch mob.
They pounded and pounded the head
Of a crocodile. Resilient victim,
It kept swirling from pain, helpless.
More children came, some adept
Only as spectators.
(They are the worse kind).
Wretchedly, they stared, but did nothing.
(Poverty is a terrible disease.
It magnifies the urge for cruelty).

A brave boy held the crocodile
By the tail. The poor creature swirled
And swirled, trying to escape.
The boy was tenacious, refused
To let the poor soul go.
The mob kept smashing its head.
Blood gushed from its nostrils and mouth.

The crocodile tried to mount
A defense, opening its mouth
And gnashing its teeth.
It tried to go after the boy,
Holding its rugged tail.
But one defenseless soul
Against a mob is
Sinking David against Goliath.
(It instilled not fear in the mob.
It only spurred their excitement).

Children threw stones; one, a club on its head.
The mob laughed and clapped.
They seemed to have a fun-filled day.

"So sad, these children," I said.
"So sad when children
Are not taught the lesson of kindness.
So sad when pain on others is fun."
"They had not imagined," I thought,
"Of being under the skin of the crocodile.
They had not imagined
That, in slaying the crocodile,
They were slaying a part of themselves."

GECKO ON THE WALL

When you see geckos
Making love on a wall,
Ask them one question,
Have you no shame?
Why eject your erotic stench
In the public? Why do you
Do it in broad daylight?
Why not wait
For the cover of night?

And, can't you fence your desires
With the primitive switches of your brains?
Have you no self-control,
Or are your desires more powerful
Than your wills's perspires?

When you see geckos
Making love on a wall,
Ask the children to run away.
For etiquette and manners still matter;
For we do not want kids
To learn too early, and
Ask uncomfortable questions.
We do not want them to
Ask probing questions
About the bedroom sports
That human-adults also do.

We do not want them
To ask vexing questions,

Such as, why do male geckos
Eject their thing so frantically
While female geckos
Sit there, so content, as if in nirvana?

A HOMELESS PERSON PICKS FOOD FROM A WASHINGTON TRASH-BIN

It is the end of the year,
And I know there are many, who do hunger bear.
For many, I know fortune has dealt a bad hand.
We must open our hands so more lives grow towards the sun.

It is the end of the year.
I know there are many silent, but on a journey of permanent tears:
The quiet birds that are homeless; the wading, wailing birds by the
    soup kitchens.
Must we bask in luxury, and gloat at our own lucks?

Must we think that we are so good,
That we never run out of shelter and food?
That we deserve all our milked lot;
While we live bottled lives, and our neighbors we forget?

I know life has effort, but is it not mostly luck?
For some have poor inheritance; some, poor starts are their luck.
We need generous hands so more lives grow towards the sun

THE WISDOM OF FIRST AND LAST

We are one from Adam.
And if you do not believe in the legend of Scriptures,
Then choose your myth. Choose Darwin.
Choose his legend of apes: how we grew from amoebae, sperms,
To our simian ancestors;
Hunting rodents and, as our brains grew, pachyderm.

And it all began in Africa, out of the void.
In the journey, we passed through *Bab-al-Mandab.*
In Africa, the seed was sown; the legend churned.
The Bushmen still keep the secrets
That we all forgot; so do the Jains of India.
We call then naked. They think the opposite.
They wear the clothes of creation,
Flesh trained to withstand the elements;
A spirit disciplined by the vibrations of the earth.
We wear the spoils of invention.
They wear the original gift.

And it seems, the more we look at them.
We learn we are one.
For what does a human need?
Food, water, straw to rest on, and the love of kin?
Spirit and stories to accompany the journey of the clock?
What else?   The rest is only the vanity of excess.

Civilization is a race to build monuments;
Erect statues, as did the pharaohs.
Invent pliant gadgets; sequester time.

And all the time saved
Moves us closer to the dust.
Civilization has led to
The extermination of brutes:
The mean-spirited plunder of
Earth-people, nature people,
Who are slow to change;
But who know a thing or two
That we do not know.
And how arrogant we can be, we the presumed civilized.
Because we can switch on the lightbulb,
And finger the iPhone, we think we are superior.

We keep squandering earth and wind
With the tireless fires of our greed.
Yet, we are not different from the savage.
Only that our desires follow our ambition.
We only know a little more algebra;
Spiced with a little alchemy.

Pinch our skin and the same blood gushes red.
We are one. The variance is in the ambition.
We have to narrow it;
To learn from the First.
For the Last humans will last only
If they discover the enduring secrets of the First.

ODE TO ASIA

Toxins spewed in the air;
Masks spread to a wide embrace.
Servile hucksters salivate for interest and profit.
History marches in rusty steps of lucre-lust.
Ah, Oriental lands!
You have heeded to the chime of mammon.
Your children pompously ride
Uncritically on the horse of progress, plundering
Other lands like your empire-predecessors, happy
With its poisons;
But the earth continues to shiver, and bleed.
You pay no heed that the earth shudders, warms.
You salivate over the lucre-lure of dark gold.

IN CHINA:
I saw the fever-pitch of commerce.
Mao's grand head hung like a colossus
In Tiananmen Square.
Beijing's residents wore mournful masks.
Progress has brought ease, but it is not cheap.
A clean future begged quietly to be heard.
But the tyranny of factories had won the day.

Skyscraper upon skyscraper, beltway
Upon beltway, Beijing is a maze of concrete and steel;
An ant-tunnel of architectural marvels.
Peer through the Beijing fog,
Towards the China Central Television building,
With its domineering arch, which lords over the city.
Locals call it *da kucha*—this radical tower, aptly

Shaped and called "big boxer shorts."
It is the new face of modern China, the dragon-B.B.C.

Near the Great Wall, jacarandas wept for balance.
They swayed like old men who have survived dynasties.
They had so much ancient wisdom,
They stored rings of ancient lore from forgotten dynasties.
A curious peasant drew to me for a selfie.
He was a sucker for connections.
Not a xenophobe, he loved building bridges;
Scorned the tyranny of walls.
In my nostalgic remembrance, I said:

> *Peasant, peasant. I remember you.*
> *Your heart was pure jade.*
> *You were open to the unfamiliar,*
> *And welcoming to the stranger;*
> *You made me hopeful.*

IN PHILIPPINES:
I saw in Manila jeepneys* release fumes from their antique exhausts.
Young men in mopeds and street peddlers with wares inundated the
    streets;
Some breathed the ruinous air; some covered their noses to arrest
    the suffocating wind.
Second-hand cars spewed noxious fumes, pungent and irritating.
A street urchin said, with unrepentant surety,
 "We are the dumpster for Europe's rejects."
 I nodded in agreement, and passed on.

At the Jose Rizal* monument in Manila, the tour guide pointed to
    walls;
Massive walls, he said, built under the Spanish,
To protect Manilla from rampaging Moors.
I was impressed. The ancient rule of the Moors
In the Sulu islands, reached a pragmatic detente
With the building of walls, which enabled
The accumulation of ransacked booty

By the colonizing Spanish.
But why not now the same conviction, I asked myself,
To contain another menace, this time,
The existential threat of odious fumes?
I asked for directions.
A street peddler pointed us to the Aquino Monument.
In my nostalgic remembrance, I said:

> *The peddler was friendly*
> *Like an old acquaintance.*
> *His heart was warm as opal.*
> *And I was hopeful.*

IN BANGLADESH:
I saw in Bangladesh massive throngs of the needy.
From Dhaka airport to outside the palatial lobby of the Sonargaon,
Thousands languished with cupped hands and desperate smiles.
Skeletons rode on rickshaws, driving the affluent to *ghazal* concerts.
I saw beautiful sari-dressed women with gold earrings on their noses;
Their colorful silk headscarves pulled from chin to nose, to protect
    from car-spewing fumes.
We asked for directions.

> *A wretched beggar smiled,*
> *Bone dominating flesh,*
> *And pointed us to the hotel.*
> *Although energy struggled to meet good will,*
> *His heart was golden citrine.*
> *And I was hopeful.*

IN THAILAND:
I saw in Thailand Buddhist monks, heads cleanly shaven,
In plastic slippers, wearing orange flowing robes.
The air was dull and hazy; smog enveloped Bangkok.
I sat behind a taxi driver, who had an album of nude women next to
    him.
I maintained a puritan disinterest, and looked out,
But he kept pointing to the hotels, Dusit Thani and Oriental.

"You see, ova dere, veli big and beautiful," he pointed.
"Lats of Eulopians seek luxuri and comfat there."

I smiled, and thought that men everywhere were the same.

---

*   *Jeepneys*:   old, antique jeeps locally re-engineered by mechanics for local passenger transport in the Philippines.

*   *Jose Rizal*: a poet and polymath and nationalist hero of the Philippines revolution against Spanish colonial rule.

OF INDIA, I HAVE HOPE
FOR THE SUN

I
Of India, how I longed to visit it;
Or did I travel there in spirit
In the chariot of my dreams?

Did I sit by the Ganges and the Brahmaputra
And watch pilgrims sail deep into their *atman**,
In search of their *moksha**
In the repentant rites of centuries?

Did I see you Mahatma, the great one;
The fighter who conquered the world
By fasting;
By not firing a quiver of arrows,
But by wearing the simple, white
Toga-gown of humility.

That Mahatma, who taught the world
The enduring lesson of *satyagraha**.
Who knew that a spindle and a thread
Can defeat the depraved canons of Empire.

Did I see you Rabindranath, the Tagore,
By the date palms of Santiniketan
Proliferating the wisdom among gurus
About the enlightened path of *Brahmo Samaj**.

Of India, how I longed to visit it;
Or did I travel there in spirit

In the chariot of my dreams?

Did I see her millions, the prosperous
And the wanting,
In Calcutta and Mumbai,
Reach into that *heaven of freedom*?*

II

Of India, I have hope for the sun.
And of the rays of the sun,
Of the shadows of *Dalits* merging with the *Brahmins*
In mutual empathy and regard;
Of the silhouettes of Hindus, Jews, Christians and Muslims,
Melding love into an unrecognizable whole.
Of the rich breaking bread with the poor
To form a circle of incestuous kindness.
Of men and women, breaking the miseries
Wrought by fate, to shape a virtuous destiny.

Of India, I have hope for a rising sun.

*   *Atman*: the real self, spirit or soul

*   *Moksha*: the transcendent state of the soul after being released from the cycle of reincarnation.

*   *Satyagraha*: Gandhi's philosophy of passive political resistance, of non-violence.

*   *Brahma Samaj*: a monotheistic movement in Hinduism which was started in Calcutta in 1828 by the reformer, Ram Mohun Roy. Tagore's father was a leader in this movement.

*   *Heaven of freedom*: a line borrowed from Tagore's famous poetry collection, *Gitanjali*.

SEASON OF VENGEANCE

It is the season when death visited us with a vengeance.
Corona crowned itself the king of the earth.
Hospitals roiled with the drama of masks and ventilators.
We heard the politicians adorn their lies with numbers.

We did not believe humanity was so fragile.
All accumulated knowledge seemed like a scandalous dungheap.
Italy and Spain bled like the era of Neanderthals.
We knew we had been careless about things that really mattered.

It is the season when death visited us with a vengeance.
Corona crowned itself the king of the earth.
Wuhan became notorious for the birth of a scourge.
Mortuaries lay overwhelmed by
The rapid march of death's spell.

They said it all started from bats.
Pathogens and viruses flew into wet markets.
History got altered by the scourge of the tiny.
China got blamed for being so secretive.
Arrogance, if not tempered, is venom for the world.

It is the season when death visited us
With a vengeance.
March became the ugliest month.
Stock markets crashed like jumbo planes.
Workers stretched their arms to the skies.
Parliaments panicked, and acted with fright.
Central Banks pumped money like crazy.

We knew we had been careless
About things that really mattered.
Greta* warned us, but, hey, did we listen?
The earth is one; emissions must sink.
But the world blocked its ears,
And continued with business. Pests jumped,
And found free rein.
Arrogance, if not tempered, is poison for the world.

 It is the season when death visited us
With a vengeance.
Corona crowned itself the king of the earth.
And we all prayed for the first time
For we were frightful.
We knew we had been careless
About things that really mattered.

---

*   *Greta Thunberg*: the young Swedish environmental activist who warned global
       leaders and ordinary citizens to take action to arrest the growing existential
       crisis from climate change.

WASHINGTON

Washington,
If you can find only one honest man;
If you can find only a man who keeps his promise;
If you can find only a man who is not a lobbyist;
If you can find only a man who is not a lawyer,
Then I know you are blessed.

If you walk towards the Capitol;
If you can find no homeless person;
If you can find no person begging for a dollar;
If you can find no vendor selling t-shirts, gloves or umbrellas;
If you can find no vendor selling hot dogs in buns,
Then I know you are blessed.

If you walk towards the Farragut Metro,
If you can find no pigeons scrounging for food droppings;
If you can find no street juggler or street drummers playing go-go
   music,
If you find no teenager diving through pedestrian and traffic with a
   skateboard;
If you find no cops with blue lights on, scouting for lawbreakers,
Then I know you are blessed.

If you pass through DuPont circle;
If you find no parked car with a parking ticket;
If you find no clusters of pigeons with necks cocked surveying
   pedestrians;
If you can find no gays or lesbians pushing their freedom,
Then I know you are blessed.

If you walk towards Adams Morgan;
If you do not see a Latino woman pushing a baby on a stroller;
If you do not see an African American man with a rasta hair;
Feeling despondent about the "system;"
If you do not hear *merengue* or *rumba* or *salsa* music,
Or jazz or reggae or rap music booming from restaurants or
    nightclubs;
If you do not see a "colored person" making the moves,
Then I know you are blessed.

If you walk to Sixteenth Street;
If you do not see clusters of Caucasians heading to restaurants;
If you pass Harvard Street heading to Silver Spring,
And head to the leafy Gold Coast;
If you do not see African Americans and Hispanics walking with
    kids;
Or a few Caucasians walking their dogs;
If you do not see churches, synagogues or mason temples,
Their congregants chit-chatting on their steps;
If you do not know God resides in the Sixteenth Street surburb in
    Washington;
If you do not see a few Ethiopians, colorfully dressed in *lemlems*,
Walking down the steps of the Ethiopian Orthodox church,
Then I know you are blessed.

If you walk back towards the White House;
If you can find no lobbyist dressed in immaculate suit and tie;
If you can find no biker with sports gear heading to a Starbucks;
If you find no tourist holding a city map;
If you can find no traffic jam on Pennsylvania Avenue,
Then I know you are blessed.

If you walk to Chinatown;
If the architecture does not remind you of the Wong Tai Sin Temple
    of Hong Kong,
Or the palatial buildings of the Forbidden City;
If the colors of red, yellow and white do not lift your spirit;

If the *paifang* arch does not invite you in its majesty;
If the hundreds of food seekers do not impress you,
Then I know you are not blessed.

When you detour to Georgetown;
If you can find no woman carrying a designer bag;
If you can find no university students feasting around beer tables;
If you can find no long-legged model looking privileged and chic;
If you can find no chic boutique with mannequins and stylish
    saleswomen,
Then I know you are blessed.

When you head to Massachusetts Avenue,
If you can find no office with a diplomatic flag;
If you can find no portion of the road without potholes;
If you pass through Mass Avenue without hearing a foreign accent;
If you can pass the Washington mosque and not see multinational
    flags on its lawn
And long bearded devotees, in genuflection, salaaming in prayer;
If you can pass through it without tourists staring at a Gandhi or a
    Churchill or a Nelson Mandela,
Then I know you are blessed.

When you head towards the Vice President's residence,
Before you reach the National Cathedral,
If you do not find armed police guards by its gate;
If you do not find tourists laying wreath on the tomb of Khalil Gibran;
If you do not see squirrels or deer foraging in the green;
If you do not see a protester holding a poster against sexual predators
    in the Catholic Church;
If you do not see the Finnish Embassy with solar panels and green
    plants preparing for Climate Change,
Then I know you are blessed.

Most importantly about Washington,
If you can visit it without a parking ticket;
If you do not hear about the escapades of Marion Barry,

The mayor of perfect convictions, but flawed as Robin Hood;
If you do not visit all those wretched whores on Georgia Avenue;
If you do not smell like car smoke after taking the metro;
If you have not encountered the humid summer heat of Foggy
  Bottom;
If you did not hear about *Ling-Ling* and *Hsing-Hsing*,
And other pandas at the D.C. zoo;
If you do not encounter a single beggar or homeless by the metro
  gate,
Then I know you are truly blessed.

So, count your blessings after visiting Washington.
For you have seen the world.
You have seen the world's perfections and imperfections.
If you chose, you may go to no other place.

NASTY PALAVER OF DONALD DUCK*

I.
He said we are people from the shit-hole continent,
He does not know us, but wealth and ignorance
Can breed insolence from a drake, holding the scepter.

But if his claim is true, then we must have drakes, like him, shitting
     on us.
But *does he really know us?* I don't know.
The life of golf courses and grabbing ducks,
The heaving entitlement of a thoughtless neanderthal;
The discharge of the tongue before the brain is engaged.
God, save us from bluster of the privileged tongue.

II.
Because he said what he said,
When we climb on planes, people look at us.
Some don't want to sit near, because they are unsure.
Some simply smile, but want to sit far.
Some jump straight and say, "Hello!
Must be an ordeal to come out of a hole
Where many shit on you? I am surprised you do not stink.
Did you put on cologne?"
I smile, saying only, "Thank you!"
For what else can one say
If, as he claims, we are from a shithole.

Even those from worse shit-holes, they hold their noses.
They turn their faces, when they see you.
You hold your head high, and pretend you are not

Seeing anybody. You wish they have minimum decency
To leave you alone. But there is no peace,
Since he* said we are people
From the shit-hole continent.
Even though *he really does not know us.*

III.
You ask, who is doing the shitting,
If we are a shit-hole continent? And how large is his anus?
For we are catching too much of his shit,
And I have to tell you, it is foul and sad.
Sometimes we see his anus so big
For he is obese, and has overeaten.
We say, "wow, we are going
To catch a lot of shit."

IV.
Man, I say to the drake, please, have mercy on us.
Since you claim we are the shit-hole continent.
I repeat, "Have mercy on us." And we also pray,
"May God teach you love and respect."
But if you do not believe in God,
"May whatever you believe in teach you some humility."

We also urge you that, once in a while, please take some rest, and eat
    less.
For we know too much food sometimes jaundices the mind.
For the earth is suffering from such unbridled
Arrogance and greed. So, a bit of empathy
Might even make the earth better breathe.

---

*   On Sept 26, 2018 of *Newsweek,* it was reported that Trump asked, "Why are
we having all these people from shithole countries come here?" Reference was
to immigrants from Haiti, El Salvador and African countries to the US. His
complaint-- a shortlist of poor countries that export immigrants, a **shit-hole
countries redux**, so to speak. It is **not hard to imagine the long list**. Lost
to him was America's founding ideals of it being a nation of immigrants and

the enormous contributions made by immigrants to America's economy and society. American is great and exceptional because America replenishes itself through immigration. Ronald Reagan, that arch republican, recognized that and spoke about it. Lost to Trump (reflecting his own ignorance of American history) was the Emma Lazarus inscriptions under the Statue of Liberty, *"Give me your tired, your poor, your huddled masses yearning to breathe free. The wretched refuse of our teeming shore."*

MIDLIFE

Midlife is an island with quaint questions.
I approached it with anticipation, but dreaded its implications.
Thoughts came afloat, of those that I knew
Who died young. The fortunes of life
Shudder, like that of a bird that seizes grains
But then loses them in mid-flight.

I remember many I knew who were angels
But fell to the axe of the grim-harvester.
Where is Solo Manneh or Kalamanlie Juwara?
Where is Sam Njie?
I ask, why they? It seems the answer
Is as meaningful as why lizards fall from a mango tree.
I have ceased contemplating
The meaning of life. If you have an answer,
Please tell the Rabbi, Pope, or Imam.
They are prayerfully looking for it.

I am not a jester, and not a philosopher.
They have their trades, and perhaps that gives
Them meaning. I am an ordinary soul
Who has gone through the meandering streams
Of life, and sometimes wonder, why me?
I am thrown into this world,
Like everyone else. Was I consulted?
Thrown like a ball
Into the lottery of an ineluctable game.
I am kicked by the wind, drenched by the rain, and
Abused by the sand.
I am like the gamboling antelope

On the Savannah landscape, that maneuvers
Between predators and prey, between hyenas and grass.

What I know is that midlife is an island.
And Only I, know my solitary anguish.
Memories rack my mind. Sometimes,
Memory burns bright as bougainvillea;
But other times, it flops hazy as dawn.
Sometimes, memory is painful
As touching charcoal embers.
I swing along, sometimes propelling my mind
Into the warm revelry of dreams.
I think of bright-starred heavens; riotous lights.
Sometimes I simply let my brain
Become a spaceship of enchantments.

GROWING OLD

I am leaking gas.
I am growing old.
White hair is growing all over me.
It is the cotton syndrome.
First, I grew a bulge.
Then I began to forget
Where I placed my keys.
Then I began to accuse my children;
Then I find my keys
And my lips turn into
An altar for apologies.

I am growing old.
My long memory is sharp as a razor,
But my short memory is dull as a fog.
I like to take walks
And see childless women walk their dogs
Scooping poop with a plastic grocery bag
Like proud moms.

Loneliness is a terrible malady.
And if you do not believe me,
Ask the desolate cactus in the Sahara.
Just walk the middle class-streets of America
On a weekday mid-morning.
You will see childless women
With poodles and pugs on a leash,
Holding cellphones, and screaming unpleasantries
At the late maintenance man.

Or could it be that they are lonely women
Tending an empty nest.
Ah, don't be on the receiving end
Of a lipstick on a lonely woman walking a dog....
They can be fierce as a pit-bull.
Even the police fear
The rage of lonely women.

Only poodles and pugs,
Reared slowly as gentle breeds,
Have the temper for their rage.
Only poodles and pugs,
Have stomachs, fortified enough,
To keep them company.

Did I forget what I was talking about?
This is because I am growing old.
And my short-term memory is failing me
Like a diaper fails a tottering baby.
It is not my fault.
I do all the right things.
I eat broccoli, collard greens and tomatoes.
They say, tomatoes help men
Because of the lycopene.
I go to bed early
And try to have a good pact with my bed.
I avoid cellphones, iPads,
And all those ghastly devices
Invented by the internet thugs
To keep us busy from each other.
All those little toy-spies,
That invade our pillows like bedbugs.
That my wife loves to bring along.

I am growing old.
Chipmunks drill tunnels under my house.
They know I am too slow to run after them.

So, they do the cat-and-mouse.
I am the cat,
And they are the mice.
But they know I am a slow cat;
I can't compete.
They are like children,
Naughty scoundrels.
They eat all my flowers.
But I have retired from babysitting.

And worse are the groundhogs.
Cowards they are;
Fearful at any minor screech.
They quickly dash away for cover.
Lovely they can be
When they stand on two legs
Like our bi-pedaling ancestors.

In my backyard, they are multiplying like mushrooms.
Except they are not annuals.
They are like invasive perennials.
Do they know that
I am growing old?
That I am gaining slowly
The mettle to face my loneliness?
I am leaking gas.
I am leaking gas.
The elements are
Taking over me.
I am growing old.

COME, BE MY FRIEND

Mint in black tea.
Come to the table
And be my friend.

Sugar not needed.
Only a tongue
That can taste and tell.
Come to the table
And be my friend.

The irrevocable delight
Of sumptuous friendship.
A kettle lifted;
Hot water bubbling.
Come to the table
And be my friend.

Hold your china,
See the leaves boil;
Salivate with anticipation.
Come to the table
And be my friend.

Few things in life
Are laced with sweetness.
Few, so riddled with joy,
As friends, unburdened
By marsh-worries.
So come to the table
And sip from

The gourd of calmness.

Come,
And be my friend.

WHEN THE SKY IS
ABOUT TO FALL

When the sky is about to fall on our heads,
What do we say or do before God?
Should we kneel, or stand?
So what must we do?
Twitter like midget-birds into the boundless heavens?
Fight back, or wait for the overpowering abyss?

Is there hope if we do not stand
In the verity of verities, the silence in the onion core?
Is this core wisdom, the tiny that is massive,
Or the massive that is tiny,
As when the universe returns to its seed, or
As when sun fragments unsettle the heavens?

Maybe we should stand
And dig our feet deep into peat.
Stand confident in the faith of things small;
Pretend like vetiver grass
That all that matters is roots.

If the heavens rumble
To test the pebbles in our hearts,
Should we mutter the monotonous chants,
The desperate psalms of the agnostics:
We never knew;
We never knew?

Of course, the Angel would say,
What happened to the Faith of your Fathers?

What happened to the slow, sure dogmatic truths,
Filled with the snail's cautious move,
Shoved like jello through
Your savage throats?

Can we say:
We never knew?

For we had Pascal's gamble,
So clever; so geometrical.
And the mad men of the Scriptures.
And the tireless women of example.
We had Mother Teresa.
And luckily a lifetime long enough
To foreclose our doubts.

ELEGY FOR DR. LENRIE PETERS

Earth, receive an honored guest;
Lenrie Peters is laid to rest.
Let the Gambian vessel lie
Emptied of its poetry*.

In the blaze of a summer sky,
The Katchikalli-sage departed from us.
Leaving young and old admirers sad.
Never again to hear his Cambridge-voice.

After a sting of illness taut with despair,
Our beloved surgeon ended up in Dakar.
All his medical lore gave no relief.
Our dear friend succumbed at Dantec*.

Diabetic pains lingered long in his veins.
Addiction to whisky and cigar
Corroded away slowly
At his radiance and stamina.
He savored music from all climes.
And tuned his ears daily to the BBC.

Of his love for The Gambia,
Seldom can there be doubt.
He loved the country like dolphins loved its river.
He also loved his well-knit clothes;
Embroidered tie-dye and *cubavera* suits.
Of his demeanor, he was pinned
To quietness and reserve.
If you tickled him, he gave
That sneaky belly-laugh.

He was bitter with complaints,
Unrelenting in his disgust,
And slashing in his rage.
For crooked politicians, he had no relief.
Jammeh *, he said, was a kleptocrat
Through and through, colorful with antics,
But sadly shepherded our peaceful country
Into a hollering slaughterhouse.

Earth, receive an honored guest;
Lenrie Peters is laid to rest.
Let the Gambian vessel lie,
Emptied of its poetry.

---

*   Lines borrowed from Auden's elegy for Irish poet, W.B. Yeats.

*   *Dantec*: Hospital in Dakar.

*   *Jammeh*: the deposed dictator of the Gambia (1994-2016).

ELEGY FOR CHINUA ACHEBE

Dear teacher, as we ponder your Exit,
We know a weighty star in our sky has left us.
Our bruised hopes seek your soaring light.
At the edge of clouds, we stare. We mourn.

Dear teacher, it cannot be the same.
You were the luminous light from Ogidi.
We drew to you because we believed your lore.
In this, our twilight of loss, that Fate,
So cruel, stole you, when so unexpected,
We will remember you for your dreams to make Africa fly;
Your light to illuminate the untruths about Africa.
We will remember your integrity and your spine.

Now that you are suddenly gone, dear brother,
Who will tell us where the rain began to beat us?
Who will give us cultural hope to overcome our impediments?

Dear teacher, now that we have lost you,
Someone else must bear your weight.
And, now, as we ponder your Exit,
A heavy sadness squats in our hearts.
We will not let it go--
Until Africa awakens to your wisdom.

ELEGY FOR NADINE GORDIMER

The anti-apartheid wasp with the bite of steel.
The scribbler with a pen, fiercer than an assegai.
Your father came prospecting for gold in Egoli.
He produced a diamond in you.

You were not muffled by cruel edicts of censorship.
You loved truth like your birth.
Did they know Lithuania wedded to Britain
On the Cape—gave birth to a voice of steel?
Did they know how you loathed injustice?

Your ancestors escaped the cruel anguish from Europe;
Then how could they return to it in the serenity of the Cape?
You were no ostrich, no back-bencher, that buried its head
In the Kalahari sand. No embracer of vile nationalism.

You took your pen and charged it
With the tip of stubborn steel, and exuded
A combative spirit, turbo-charged with
The grace of a menacing wisdom.

Comrade—as you liked to call your friends—
We knew this was no cheap vanity-stunt.
We knew this was conviction, commitment.
Like fellows on the eucharist, we knew you were vested
In the bond of enduring solidarity.

Comrade, I remember our last lunch,
At your leafy green home at Parktown West.
Raks Sekhoa was there. You gave me a signed Zulu album,

And a signed copy of your recent novel.
Such civilities mark the routine of writers.
And then you treated us to a feast of salad and salmon sandwiches.

I did not know it would be the last time
I will ever see you, valiant friend.
I did not know. But I still remember
Your obdurate love of truth.
I still remember your love for justice.
I still remember your radiant soul.
You were a petite bird that moved mountains.

You flew, but have not left, dear Sister.
Like Mandela, you ignited light and love over South Africa.

MEDITATION ON WHITE HAIR

When age creeps on your head, pulsing in the faint glimmer of white
hair,
Count your blessings for being among the lucky ones.
Avoid pettifogging; spend the remaining time in goodness.
For there is recompense for deeds here, after you have crossed the
river.

And if you think, being a sacerdotal minion is quackery,
That there is no grace; no celestial gate;
Then as a flagbearer of this world; still count your blessings,
And at least acknowledge that waters sweet and muddy
Have passed through this boisterous earth
To the sweet Unknown that placed you here.